CW01654725

Process and Prosper

Why it's essential to cry, stamp your feet and get angry and how it can save your life.

For information about Wendy Harrington's work visit her website at www.wendy-harrington.com

Process and Prosper

....

A guide for your inner journey

....

Wendy Harrington

First edition published in 2010
© Copyright 2010
Wendy Harrington

The right of Wendy Harrington to be identified as the author of this work has been asserted by her in accordance with the Copyright, Designs and Patents Act 1998.

All rights reserved. No reproduction, copy or transmission of this publication may be made without express prior written permission. No paragraph of this publication may be reproduced, copied or transmitted except with express prior written permission or in accordance with the provisions of the Copyright Act 1956 (as amended). Any person who commits any unauthorised act in relation to this publication may be liable to criminal prosecution and civil claims for damage.

Although every effort has been made to ensure the accuracy of the information contained in this book, as of the date of publication, nothing herein should be construed as giving advice. The opinions expressed herein are those of the author and not of MX Publishing.

Paperback ISBN 9781907685033
Published in the UK by MX Publishing
335 Princess Park Manor, Royal Drive,
London, N11 3GX
www.mxpublishing.co.uk

Contents

Acknowledgements

Thank you to all who have been involved in making this book possible, especially Rachel Sampson and Kathryn Hudson. A special thank you to my loving partner Kevin, you were a key person in saving my life and now I am so grateful that you are part of my life every day.

Thanks to all my family, especially my Mum and wonderful daughters. You all teach me so much.

To try and thank everyone who was involved in my amazing medical care would be impossible. There are names that stand out but those people are supported by a host of unseen people. Every single person is important in a team and my gratitude goes to you all.

Foreword

Sudden critical illness and a near death experience awakened me to the knowledge that there is not only life after death, but also much more to the world than we can see.

This book is the story of my journey of self discovery so far. It is my exploration to live my life with more peace, calm and happiness, which ironically I have found by allowing, accepting and feeling sadness and anger.

My experience has been that it is a tough challenge to wake up to life. It takes courage and determination to go beyond conditioned thought patterns and beliefs. It is a journey well worth taking though. The rewards are huge.

It is my honour and pleasure to be part of your journey. I believe we are moving towards awareness of our connection to all others, which begins with a deeper understanding of ourselves.

This book has been deliberately written to be short, so that you can read it quickly and then re-read it as many times as you like.

About The Author

Wendy Harrington is an author, mentor, speaker and mother of 3. Since a near death experience in 2001, she has been exploring mental, physical, emotional and spiritual aspects to create a more peaceful, fulfilling and easy life. Wendy has worked with experts around the globe on spiritual awakening, mindset, Tai Chi, Chi Kung, Meditation, Photo-reading, Constellation work, Shiatsu and Psychology. In the process she found levels of peace and contentment that she had never experienced before and now works with others to help them breakthrough their limitations and experience increased peace, joy and harmony in their lives. Wendy's warm, open, honest and down to earth approach has helped her connect with thousands of people wanting to break through hidden obstacles and experience greater joy, success and harmony in life.

'Process and Prosper' is based on her personal experience of battling to recover from necrotising fasciitis following the birth of her third child. It's a story of courage, of struggle against her own fears and limitations, and the discovery of the emotional freedom available when we connect with our physical intelligence (the wisdom held in our physical bodies).

Chapter 1

The Big Jolt

On the 5th June 2001 a beautiful baby girl was born to me and my husband Ro (Roland). I didn't feel too well and had been having some contractions, so she was delivered, 8 weeks early, by emergency caesarean section. The hospital had been monitoring her heart rate and it had dipped, which meant the surgeons decided to deliver her. For 8 weeks early she was a good weight, at 4lb 8 oz, and did well in the incubator. We called her Martha Faith. I didn't feel great but put it down to having had an operation, as I had never had one before.

Gradually as the days went by my health deteriorated and I became more unwell. The fourth night following the birth I had such painful abdominal pains that I didn't know what to do with myself. I thought I had some serious constipation, but as I deteriorated further it became obvious that it was much more serious than this. On the morning of 9th June I was taken to the intensive care unit. I remember initially thinking that I had appendicitis, but as I deteriorated I thought I had meningitis; perhaps because meningitis was in the press a lot at that time and people were dying from it. I recall being really distressed that I had given it to my children and my sister's children and they were going to die. Also I had been expressing breast milk for Martha and I was paranoid that the milk I had expressed was poisonous in some way. I repeatedly said to Ro "Don't give Martha the milk. Ring the hospital and make sure they throw it away". The pain was intense in my abdomen and thankfully drugs allowed me to drift away.

The diagnosis was necrotising fasciitis. More commonly known as the flesh eating bug, the disease is exactly as it says 'death of the tissue'. It cannot be cured and the only form of treatment is to remove any infected tissue. The surgeons removed my womb, ovaries and a large area of flesh from my abdomen and up the sides of my body. My body was overwhelmed by toxins from the flesh breaking down and gradually organs began to stop functioning properly. My bowel was perforated, my kidneys stopped working, I was on life support and losing blood as quickly as it was being pumped into my body. My heart was struggling to pump the blood around my body and so I was given drugs to help it. They also gave me drugs to keep me sedated and hoped they had removed all the disease and it wouldn't spread any further. Luckily for me they had and they used cadaveric (donor) skin as a temporary measure to seal the open wounds. The surgeons took pictures of what they had done and my poor family had to see them. They were devastated and prayed that I would survive.

It was at this time that I had the following 'near death' experience. I am floating towards a very bright light. There is stillness and a great sense of calm and peace. I am quite happily going. There are forms, but I cannot make them out clearly. Suddenly I feel a huge tug on my arm, it stops me and I am unable to go any further. I look back and it is Ro. I am holding his hand and it is as if I was pulling him behind me. I want to keep going, it is very inviting. We will go together I think. I pull harder, but I cannot move Ro and I stop pulling and look forward. I communicate with the forms (This was telepathically as I wasn't speaking words but we were having a conversation). "Can I bring Ro?" "No" is the reply. I try to go forward again anyway (I always was stubborn and it felt so wonderful that I really wanted to go) and pull Ro to come as well. I feel the tug again. I look to the forms and know that I definitely cannot take Ro. "If you come you must come on your own", they communicate. I stop. I don't want to go without Ro. So I don't go.

On Sunday 17th June the doctors reduced the sedation and woke me up. They told me everything that had happened, explaining the severity of what they had to do. They could have told me anything though because I didn't hear it at all. My first response to being told what had happened was to ask if I could just pop home and get some things for the baby and was it ok if I just had a quick shower. It could have been that my brain was so addled from the drugs that it just didn't compute, but it could also have been self protection. I have seen along my journey that I hear what I am able to hear and I really didn't want to hear that!

It took several days for the severity of what had happened to sink in as reality. My poor family had to keep telling me, because I would ask what had happened. This was really hard for them to hold it together and tell me, but I just couldn't hear it, then they would have to go through it all over again. Finally, after a few days of denial I asked Ro what had happened and he drew it out on the mega sketcher (I had this to write on because I couldn't speak due to a tracheostomy). I recall sinking into despair, I felt so ill that I just asked for more morphine to escape the emotional and physical pain… I couldn't deal with it.

Over the days that followed the surgeons took me to theatre and began grafting the exposed areas with skin from my thighs. Gradually I plucked up the courage to have a look at myself. The area was so large that the dressings were done in stages and one day I peeked at the top right hand side of me. It was so ugly I couldn't bear it, angry and red, with a step-like wedge of skin where my own body merged with this alien body that was not mine. I cried and cried and couldn't imagine how I would cope with it. More operations followed to seal my body. I had a hole in my tummy where some of my bowel (called a fistula) was protruding (this bit of bowel was protected by a bag-like covering). I also had an ileostomy (just below my sternum) which is where a portion of the small intestine is bought to the surface of your skin to allow stool collection in a stoma bag (plastic bag), thus resting the rest of the bowel so that it could heal. I hated both of these.

I spent 6 weeks on the intensive care ward, with more operations to seal my body, before being moved to the plastic surgery ward. This was the first point that I began to feel vaguely like my old self. I have fond memories of watching Quincy in the afternoons and my 2 older girls (aged 7 & 5 who were staying with their dad) coming to see me. I missed them dreadfully and they were so scared by my appearance while on the intensive care ward, that it had been really heart breaking to see their sad, scared, worried little faces. It was getting easier for them and although the younger one was still very frightened, the older one was more forward. I loved to see them, but did find the visits exhausting and felt bad that I had so little to give to them.

My Mum was able to come and stay which was such a miracle. She had taken Martha home and was doing a fantastic job of looking after her. She would bring her in every day to see me. She was always dressed in the most beautiful clothes and everyone was admiring her gorgeous pram. This was also very hard as I longed to be the one pushing the pram, cooing over her and taking care of her needs. I think it would have been even harder if she had been my first child. The fact that she was my third child bought comfort in some ways, because I knew that we would bond together as soon as I was well enough. Due to the hole in my tummy I couldn't sit up and was still bedridden and so although I did feed her with the bottle, it was awkward and tiring.

About 10 weeks after the first operation, the surgeons did the final operation to repair the bowel and close the hole in my tummy. They had wanted to send me home with the stoma and fistula so that I could get stronger. I was really keen for them to do the operation, however, because I had had a whole month of feeling sick all the time. They agreed to move it forward because of this.

The hole had resulted from the destruction of the peritoneum (the membrane that forms the lining of the abdominal cavity and basically holds the bowel in place and stops it protruding) and the surgeons needed to use something to replace the lost tissue. They used a fantastic substance called Permacol which is made from pig skin (manufactured to be compatible with human tissues) to seal in the bowel and then created a flap of skin and muscle from my thigh to close the hole.

The operation was successful and gradually I began to sit up, which was awful initially. I couldn't believe that something as simple as sitting could make me feel so violently ill. I also began to eat proper food again, as I had been on food solution which was intravenously administered. This was also really challenging, the doctors wanted me to eat loads and get lots of calories (needed for healing and repairing tissues) but I had a very low appetite and could only eat a very small amount and keep it down.

On my 30th birthday (12 weeks after being admitted to the intensive care unit) I went home for the day. It was exhausting, but great and I felt so much better at home. I returned to hospital that night, but the next day I went home for good. My 2 older girls came home and my healing continued.

This recovery period has been very difficult, dealing with physical, emotional and psychological pain and trauma. Yet it has also been one of the most rewarding periods of my life. I want to share some of the things that I have discovered, in the hope that others may benefit. The journey has, and continues to be, a fascinating one and the discoveries are relevant, not just for recovery from illness but for anyone who wishes to embrace themselves fully and live an inspired life.

Chapter 2

A Shift in Awareness

The first discovery came from the near death experience. This shift appears to be two things but these two things are one and the same. First I nearly died! There is nothing like facing your own mortality for a serious wake up call. The second thing is 'there is something else'. We are more than our physical bodies. This jolted me out of my 'we are born, we die, we are dust' way of thinking and awakened a curiosity in me.

I don't really know why, but I got drawn to Eastern philosophy for my healing. This opened up the world of energy in my body and the world. To me it's very real, because I have a direct experience of it. The first experience came in January 2003 when I began practising Tai Chi and Chi Kung. I was honoured to come across an oriental teacher, who was well connected with his own energy, and was passionate about awakening it in his students as well. I was performing a Chi Kung exercise when I suddenly felt this strong buzzing sensation in my hands and arms, as strong as if you were to hold a mobile phone in your hands that was vibrating. "What the ****?" I thought. After calming down, I realised that it was my energy. I could not believe that I had been ignorant to it for 30 years. I continued with the Chi Kung and Tai Chi, started a training course in Shiatsu, (at that point purely for my own recovery, as my body was so fragile), and started to sit in a meditation circle and explore spirituality.

I went on a Tai Chi weekend workshop in the summer of 2003. The group walked to Whistmans Wood on Dartmoor. Whistmans Wood is a phenomenally beautiful spot, with knarled stunted oaks and an abundance of mosses and lichens. On arriving we were asked to sit in silence and eat our lunch. I have to say initially it was a painful experience, my head was so busy and I longed to talk. After some gesturing and inner giggling with my friends (I guess it took me back to being at school and not being allowed to talk!), I did settle and went and sat on a rock by myself. The rock was covered in mosses and it was really soft to sit on. I found myself examining the various lichens and mosses; they were so intricate and delicate. I suddenly realised how strong the moss I was sitting on was. When I got up, it would spring back up again: if I was to have the proportionate weight on me, it would squash me. Whilst carrying out an exercise where we were 'connecting energetically' with a tree, I had the most overwhelming sense of peace and love. From this feeling came the most fundamental respect, love and feeling of unity and oneness with nature. I always knew that nature was alive, but previously had this perception of nature and me as two separate things. This experience really made me **feel** the life in nature and the oneness of life. This feeling arose spontaneously from within. It was a truly beautiful experience and at the time made me laugh to myself about the hippies in the 60's: peace and love man! I recall feeling quite spaced by the whole experience.

This experience confirmed two things for me. Firstly, it was another direct experience that there is something greater than myself, a Universal Source of energy, light, wisdom, God, call it what you will and this greater thing is Love. Not the contracted love that has conditions to it, but an expanded all encompassing non-judgemental love. The second thing is that **life is spiritual because there is no separation**. Within each of us is an inner yearning for unity, because it is our natural state and we have been blinded into believing that we are separate. That is why the way we currently live in separateness causes us so much pain. There is an inner yearning for unity, a longing to be complete. Human Nature is not as selfish as you may have been led to believe as a 'fact'. Human Nature is love.

Energy

I realise I have come to think of life very much in terms of energy and I feel it is a very important topic. I am enjoying exploring and playing with it. Energy is all around us, in all matter and all species. We are more than our perception of just physical beings, we are also energy beings. We interact and communicate on an energy level all the time, but for most of us this is unconscious. To make it conscious by expanding our own awareness of ourselves is an invaluable gift for harmonious living. Energy operates on all levels. Not only do we communicate on an individual level, we also interact in a much wider sense. Consider group atmospheres which you have been in. There can be a very different quality to the atmosphere depending on the group of people and the topic of conversation. Consider the way a particular environment makes you feel…The common phrase 'you could cut the atmosphere with a knife' talks of the sensation of energy.

In order to become more aware of energy, slow down. Take time to reflect and totally observe your interactions with other people, places and things. There are many wonderful practices to choose from to help you connect with life's energy, such as Tai Chi, Chi Kung and Yoga. There are also many simple things you can do yourself, such as slowing down or steady deep breathing.

My experience of the appreciation of energy in the world was the sudden awareness of the 'life' in all things. With this realisation came a magical feeling of just how awesome life is, coupled with a great sense of joy and humour. When I forget this and become involved in my separate self again, lost in the trappings of my closed mind, it's great to be reminded of it because I get to experience the joy of it all over again ☺

Stillness

It is time to slow down.

Life is what happens while you are busy….

One of the most important studies we can undertake in life is self-study. Getting to know ourselves is essential if we are to attain lasting peace and joy. In our material society many of us search for happiness outside of ourselves, but lasting happiness comes from within. In order to get to know yourself it is important to enter the stillness found within. In our society we are very busy and everything is fast, we are used to doing and not just being. The busier you are (both physically and mentally) the more difficult it is to reach this still calm place. From this place we can learn to see without eyes and hear without ears. In a state of deep relaxation we can connect with ourselves and the universe, enabling us to cultivate a deep sense of inner peace. Every day we are bombarded with information for our minds to organise. Many people rush around trying to achieve far more than is practical. By stilling your mind and reducing the external stimuli you create a place for inner peace to grow. It is not about emptying your mind, or seeing great visualisations, but it can be. It is what is right for you. There are no right and wrong ways, only ways. You have to find the way that suits you. It all depends on what you wish to achieve. Being still allows you to be in the now, right here, this moment. We are often preoccupied with past and future and forget about now.

Living 'now' is really beneficial. Bring all your awareness to this exact moment. Absorb the noises, smells, sensations all around you. Take a deep breath and allow your body to relax as you exhale. Do it now…!

It also works well to focus on something and bring all your awareness to that thing. For example, look at a flower and bring all your awareness to your observation of the flower, see in great detail all the intricate qualities and design. From this state of presence your awareness will naturally expand.

I live more of my life in this way, but still get sucked into the goings on at various points. Whenever I feel I have lost my way and find myself beginning to worry about things in the future I consciously bring my awareness to 'now'. I find a spontaneous peace and the melting of any worry or anxiety, gratitude for all that I have returns and an appreciation of the beauty of nature. I find it works really well to dispel anything I may have been fretting over.

Living life in the now does not mean that you cannot think about or plan for the future. It just means don't get lost fretting over what might happen in the future. This is a product of the mind, a trap if you like.

Meditation is the most commonly known way to enter stillness. There are many physical and emotional benefits of meditation that have been scientifically proven, such as reduced stress, sharpened intuition, increased creativity, more inner peace and discovering your potential. The traditional sitting cross-legged is not compulsory, however as your practice develops, various postures can help with the energy flow within your body. Sit however you are comfortable, maybe on a chair, or you could lie on the floor. Sitting can help to keep the mind from becoming sleepy.

The mind is very busy and when you initially attempt to still it, it may appear to be even busier. Your mind may rush with thoughts. Don't try to push them away, simply acknowledge them and allow them to pass. They will not go anywhere and you can deal with them later. My mind is very active, but I have found that it is much clearer. It is still very active, although it doesn't seem to run away with itself like it used to....well not as much anyway ☺ I think a number of things have changed, not just meditation, but a whole package, such as changing awareness, perception and beliefs. It makes sense to me that there is never just one thing, because the importance is in finding balance.

In my experience meditation can be quite different. I have participated in many meditations where I feel I have connected with something greater than me. Others where I have almost been a little disappointed that nothing miraculous has happened, but then later realised that I was totally relaxed and peaceful which is pretty miraculous in itself for many of us!

You do not have to meditate. Stillness can be found by slowing down and doing basically anything that doesn't demand constant evaluation from your mind or physical body. Maybe a repetitive task, such as gardening, walking or cleaning or you can use something to focus on, such as a flower.

If time is an issue then find ways to bring it into your daily life. Slow down your pace when you are walking for a bit and bring your awareness to every step you take, or do the ironing or washing up with your total attention on that task alone.

As you move further into this place of stillness within you it will become part of your daily life. You begin to realise how many things you were missing. For me it felt like taking off a pair of blinkers. This feeling/heightened sense comes and goes. I love it when I am in this space: the colours of the world appear brighter, I feel tall and calm and I notice so much more. However, there is nothing like a bit of emotional turmoil to contract myself and lose this wonderful connection, by returning to the ramblings and trappings of my mind.

Living in a Box

"Suffering is not in the fact, it is in the perception of the fact". Sri Bhagavan

We are all products of our cultural beliefs and life experiences.

As we grow, we learn about the world around us through our experiences and interactions with others. Think about it for a minute. Why do you think and behave the way you do? You didn't decide for yourself; you were taught by your parents and society: through the things you saw, and the responses to your behaviour and the things you said. How many things do you accept at face value without giving them a second thought?

Conditioning has its place, it can be a good thing. For example, when we experience something dangerous the brain sets up a pattern of response to that event to protect us in the future. However, while we are unaware that we are conditioned, we are limiting ourselves, because we react to the current experience through the lens of the past experience, rather than responding through choice.

Phobias are a good example of past conditioning in present action. Until recently, I had a fear of flying. It wasn't severe enough to be a phobia, but it did make me feel very uncomfortable on a plane. I was flying somewhere with my sister and I chose to share my fearful thoughts. This was therapeutic in itself, as sharing our innermost thoughts can highlight just how unrealistic they are. This can often clear the limiting thoughts and allow greater expansion. I shared that I had thoughts of the plane landing by heading nose first towards the ground. She laughed and it made me realise how daft this was. As I allowed myself to feel my fear and acknowledged that is not how planes land, an old memory surfaced of the first time I had flown. The airport was in a built up area and required a steep decent to land. I could see how I had created a pattern in my thinking and body from this experience and carried it forward onto every flight. Since sharing and feeling my fears, I have been on one flight. I felt much calmer and far more relaxed. As if to test me, one of the landings was on a very windy day and the plane was being buffeted around. The lady next to me was really scared and I ended up holding her hand to comfort her. Previously, that would have been me.

This repeating of the same behaviour only leads to more of the same and so if we are unhappy about where we are in our lives we may think there is nothing we can do about it. In order to view things with a fresh perspective you need to see that you are a product of your past, you are a product of your conditioning. I find it so liberating to embrace the fact that I am completely conditioned. Somewhere in this realisation is freedom.

This is not about blame. Our parents, teachers and society do the best they can with the information that they have available to them at the time. If you find it hard to accept this, then perhaps look at it this way instead: you are the one who is being hurt by blaming someone else and therefore only keeping yourself stuck. You deserve to be free, so do yourself a favour and choose to move on.

It takes courage and determination to go beyond conditioned thought patterns and beliefs. Many of these beliefs do not come from the current generation alone but are many years old. They are passed from one generation to the next, becoming so deeply ingrained that we accept them as facts. We move through our lives on automatic pilot, rather than realising they are choices and that we have the power to choose differently. We all live within processes and systems that we ourselves have created in order to make our lives better. **We created all these systems and processes, so we have the power to change them.**

There is always something to learn from our experiences, whether we deem them good or bad. By embracing experiences in such a way we are able to grow. Try viewing your experiences in this way. This involves taking responsibility for yourself as opposed to holding others responsible for what happens to you.

Chapter 3

Techniques for Self Empowerment and Emotional Freedom

5 Core Principles for Self Empowerment

1. Presence - Living in the moment

2. Responsibility - For your feelings, thoughts and actions

3. Resistance - What you resist persists

4. Choice - There is always a choice

5. Acceptance - Flow with life

Intellectually understanding these principles is one aspect. Truly living them is another! To be able to not just' talk the talk' but 'walk the walk' takes practice. All the core principles inter-link with, and support each other.

Maintaining Presence

When you become fully present to the moment, spontaneous joy arises within you. It does not matter what you are doing or where you are.

If you think about it the present moment is the only moment that truly exists, as anything else is the past or the future and therefore only a concept in your mind.

Most of us are either projecting into the future or reflecting on the past and are therefore not present to the moment that is happening. One of the most simple and effective tools for becoming present is to become aware of your breathing. Try it now....bring all your attention to your breathing and take rhythmic deep breaths. When you breathe deeply and smoothly your brain receives the message that the environment is safe and you can relax. On the other hand, if you take shallow breaths, the brain receives the message that there is danger and will respond by keeping your body on alert.

Breathing, to promote relaxation, is such a simple technique that can effortlessly be part of your daily life and will make a real difference to how you feel. Make the decision and commitment right now to begin this practice. At some point every day focus on your breathing, even if it's just for 5 minutes. Deepen your breath and really breathe into your whole body, allow your stomach to expand, feel your lungs filling up and your chest expanding. The more you bring your awareness to your breathing, the more your breath will deepen and the calmer and more connected, with yourself and the universe, you will become. The beauty is you don't have to put special time aside, as you can easily incorporate breathing awareness into something you already do. Washing up, driving or taking a walk. The new deeper and more relaxed breathing becomes a habit and you will naturally start to breathe more deeply all the time and become more aware when you are not fully breathing.

Responsibility

"No one can make you feel inferior without your consent". Eleanor Roosevelt (1937)

We are responsible for our own feelings and we have the capacity to choose how we feel about something. This idea can seem alien to us if we are in the habit of focusing outside of ourselves. It appears that others are responsible for our feelings. It is so common in our language and psyche to say things such as "He made me feel awful" or "She makes me feel so angry".

Learning to take more responsibility is one of the most challenging and difficult aspects, but is the only way to self empowerment and liberation.

If we focus on the outside world we give away our personal power to someone else. We cannot control others, but we can be in control of our own thoughts, feelings and actions. I know this is a hard concept to grasp. Firstly, let's be kind to ourselves. Can we really take responsibility when we do not have awareness of something? I think probably not. A good friend of mine asked me whether I felt I had a choice in being ill. This is a big question and one I don't have the answer to at the moment, and maybe never will. I'm going to use a simpler example for now. When I was 18, I shared a house with a friend. I was only there a short while before I met someone special and then spent most of my time at his house instead of my shared house. At the end of our agreement we received a huge electricity bill. There was conflict between us and I thought she was behaving unreasonably about something, the details of which are irrelevant. The upshot was I refused to pay my half of the bill and offered an amount which I thought was fair. I didn't pay her anything in the end. For years this event would niggle away at me every now and again. I would always bring it into my head and rationalise it by telling myself how difficult she was and various other things about her. One day, after years of it coming up, I started to think about it differently. It occurred to me that it didn't matter what she had done, the fact was I should have paid my half of the bill. All the uncomfortable feelings vanished when I accepted my part and took responsibility for my actions. The uncomfortable feelings in the body are messages of incongruence between our conscious and unconscious, and are our call to look inside ourselves, (more on how to do that later, in the 7 steps on page 21).

Resistance

Resistance can take many forms and can be incredibly subtle. It can be internal or external. Externally you may be refusing to accept the reality of what is happening in your current or past circumstances. Have a good look at what you are thinking about it, because "***Suffering is not in the fact, it is in the perception of the fact***". Sri Bhagavan.

One day I was out with my mum and my (then) 5 year old daughter, Martha. It was raining quite hard and we all had umbrellas. Suddenly we came across a part of the path where water was torrenting down over the whole path, meaning we had to go through it to go forward. My mum saw it and said in a distressed voice "Oh God!" but Martha squealed in delight and ran full pelt under the water with it pounding off her umbrella. My mum and I burst out laughing and the contrast between the two different reactions made it obvious to me the power of perception. It is not really what is happening but how we choose to perceive it.

Choice

When we feel we have no choice we feel powerless, yet we always have choices. It may not be an easy choice but it is there nonetheless. Accepting this links us to our internal power.

This is another really tricky one to get to grips with. Let's think about children and work as examples. We may feel that we have no choice but to care for our children or go to work. The reality is you still have a choice. You could walk away from either of these things if you chose to. The consequences might be dire and something you want to avoid at all costs but nonetheless, a choice is still being made. This can be a very empowering thing, when we feel frustrated with our children or sick of our work, by embracing that we are making the choice to care for our children or go to work, returns us to our state of personal power. Return to feeling liberated that you have chosen to wash and iron your teenagers clothes that are scattered on their bedroom floor…or better still make the choice not to! ☺

Acceptance

When we truly accept the present moment, with no resistance, we are life. True acceptance is one of the biggest challenges, it involves surrender. Not surrender to someone else but surrender to life itself. The difference with this type of surrender is that life does not want to punish you; life does not think you are bad. Life is love.

Many people have had very painful experiences in their lives and I do not detract from this in any way. However, I urge you to look at your experiences in a new way. In order to be free we need to embrace and accept our past. It is a part of us and we cannot get rid of it.

Ro and I separated in early 2007 and it was a really challenging time for me. I was the one who had instigated it, yet he was the one who was very quickly into another full time intimate relationship. This nearly drove me nuts! I resisted it with every ounce of my being, because I really didn't want to accept it. I remember him saying to me one day, "This is how it is. Just accept that." I won't use a ton of expletives to express my discontentment at this suggestion, but you get the picture. The fact is though, he was totally right. I needed to accept the situation as it was. That doesn't mean that I wouldn't have felt pain but it does mean I could have got on with processing my pain and moving forward, rather than ranting around like a spoiled child who hadn't got their way! (That makes me laugh to embrace that part of me).

Emotions that Block

Any events that happen in your life have positive or negative emotions attached to them. If not fully processed and integrated, emotions can be held within the body, mind and energy system and result in us reacting to situations rather than making an informed response.

The energy of our systems needs to flow. Suppression stops the flow, which leads to initial symptoms, such as tiredness or headaches, and in continuing circumstances may result in more serious illness.

When we don't fully process an event that causes emotion within the body and a similar experience arises, these pre-conditioned feelings emerge. The trick is to learn the patterns because often as these feelings arise we attach them to the new situation and believe that that situation or person is responsible for making us feel that way. **The only person who makes you feel in any particular way is you.** If you accept this then you begin to really liberate yourself.

As you free yourself from these old conditionings you will begin to approach life a whole new way, each experience becomes fresh and you will be able to see what is actually happening rather than what you 'think' is happening. This allows you to evaluate it for its own merit and respond in the way you choose. If you do not do this you may spend your life repeating the same patterns, often patterns that you don't want.

We sometimes hold on to old models because they are more comforting than the fear of the unknown. You may feel that you cannot let go or you may not wish to let go. Sometimes you may be unaware of the root of your problems as past traumas may be held in your unconscious. Start by choosing to move on (even if you don't know the root). It starts with a decision.

Just what does it mean letting go? How do you do it? It sounds so simple doesn't it … 'just let go'. I have found it one of the hardest things to do. I do believe that it starts with making the choice to let go. Oneness Blessing has taught me that in order to 'let go' we have to accept what is. We have to see where we are at and embrace that, warts and all. When we fully accept what is, change happens effortlessly and naturally. Fully accepting something is a challenge because we are avoiding the internal discomfort. Resisting those horrible internal feelings, you know the ones, those sinking, gut churning, tension causing, nauseating feelings which naturally cause us to run in the other direction trying to avoid them at all costs. Some feelings are easy, such as joy or happiness, which feel great in the body and we naturally expand or open to them, however, feelings such as sadness and pain feel uncomfortable and all too often we contract or close to them, putting the lid on them so to speak. Another challenging aspect is that of accepting the feelings that are labelled 'bad' in our society such as, hate, jealousy and anger. This is difficult because we are all the time resisting these feelings within us because we have been told they are not good and so we believe that we shouldn't be like that, feel like that, think like that or behave like that. Hence we are in denial of our true feelings and in denying our true feelings all we are doing is denying ourselves.

The 7 Steps to Emotional Processing

1. Own it

2. Be quiet and put the story on hold.

3. Bring it inside and see it as energy

4. Feel it

5. Breathe and invite expansion

6. Be Honest

7. Be open

1. Own it

The first step is the biggest challenge and will possibly mean changing a habit of your life so far. It ties in closely with responsibility and is about you taking ownership of your thoughts, feelings and behaviour. So begin by owning the emotion as yours, know you are choosing to have that emotion, it is not anything that anyone else is doing. People react differently to the same stimulus, for example, the thought of flying will invoke different reactions, yet it is the same concept. These differences result from our past experiences. Emotional responses can also be mood dependent, when in a good mood something doesn't bother us, but if we are in a bad mood, the very same thing can be intensely challenging. These examples point to the trigger being something inside us, rather than outside us.

Ownership is the first step to true emotional liberation, because until you do this you will not be able to fully process your emotion. All the time that you make it about someone else means that it will be impossible for it to be completed. Making it about someone else is also one of the best and most successful avoidance strategies, one we are all really good at.

The beauty of projecting our discontent onto someone else, or something else, is that it helps us to avoid our own internal discomfort, because we can bring our awareness out of our body and instead put it into our thinking. The problem is that all it does is keep us stuck, because although it may initially appear to make us feel better and enable us to 'put a lid' on the emotion, it is still there. The other thing that can happen is that we add fuel to the uncomfortable feeling by mulling it over in our thoughts, therefore keeping us in an endless cycle. At the end of the day the feelings are ours and if we really do want freedom we need to accept it as so. So stop projecting it on to someone or something else and take responsibility for your anger, sadness or annoyance. Make the choice to feel it and know that you will learn something amazing about yourself.

2. Become quiet and put the story on hold.

Ok, so you have managed to stop ranting about what an inconsiderate ******* your partner/neighbour (whoever) is, or you are trying desperately hard to stop feeling sad about how badly you feel you have been treated by someone. Now what may happen is you will start thinking about the event and try to justify your emotion as valid. This is your story and another layer of avoidance of that internal discomfort. Are you seeing a pattern here? Basically we are all running away from those difficult uncomfortable feelings that arise inside of us. True emotional liberation comes from facing these gut churning, prickly, tension creating feelings. Make the decision to feel it/connect with it and breathe smoothly and deeply. The difficult emotions, such as fear, pain and anger result in us closing to them and in a sense putting a lid on them. Anything not fully processed gets held in your body system and will keep resurfacing or worse, the effort of keeping all the emotions in your box will start to drain you of your life energy and vitality. To become a free flowing spontaneous Being, we need to open to these difficult feelings. Decide to put the story on hold and allow the emotions to guide you to the insight and wisdom you seek.

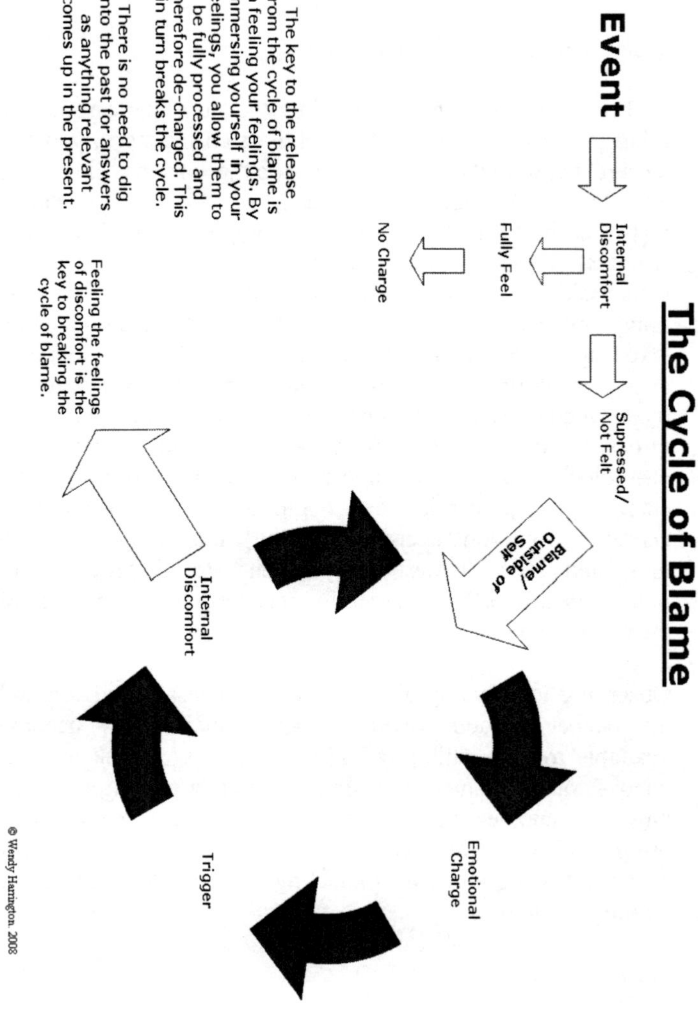
The Cycle of Blame
Event
Internal Discomfort
Fully Feel
No Charge
Supressed/ Not Felt
Blame/ Outside of Self
Emotional Charge
Trigger
Internal Discomfort
Feeling the feelings of discomfort is the key to breaking the cycle of blame.
The key to the release from the cycle of blame is in feeling your feelings. By immersing yourself in your feelings, you allow them to be fully processed and therefore de-charged. This in turn breaks the cycle.
There is no need to dig into the past for answers as anything relevant comes up in the present.
© Wendy Harrington. 2008

Blaming others and outside events keeps us stuck in a never-ending cycle.

3. Bring it inside and see it as energy

To help you stop being absorbed by the story you can do two things. Firstly, take a step back and watch the story, you can be sure that initially if you try and stop the story it will become even louder. Psychological studies of stereotypes have shown that when we try and suppress a stereotype it comes back even stronger. This will be true of your story so instead of suppressing it, allow it but don't get involved in it. The next thing you can do is instead of your mind's attention being taken up by the details of the story, turn the attention/your awareness instead to start examining your body and just where those uncomfortable feelings are. Is it your stomach, back, throat? Or anywhere else? Start watching it and in order to get past blocks, such as "I shouldn't be angry, it's not nice", change your perception and begin to see the emotion as energy….E motion (energy in motion), this energy wants to move and flow. The best way you can help this process is to breathe deeply and rhythmically, and become an observer of the energy moving in your body.

Observing in this way allows your awareness to expand and the deeper wisdom (***your*** deeper wisdom) will become available to you. This physical wisdom is your link to your unconscious. You may see a limiting thought pattern, you may move into another emotion, you may remember something that brings clarity to your problem. The possibilities are endless because this is about you connecting with your own source of guiding wisdom.

4. Feel it

Anger and tears are a natural emotional response so embrace them. Feel the anger, sadness, pain. Allow yourself to dissolve fully into it, don't buy into the 'story', keep breathing deeply and hold the feeling like you would a small child. Love it...Care for it....Accept it. There is pain and things do happen that will make us sad, but that's ok.

Moving your body can help as well because this moves energy. It opens the energy channels in the body and creates more flow. Try stretching, rotations or taping your body with your fingertips. **Remember to breathe deeply.**

Emotions are in layers, for example there is often sadness under anger, but the most beautiful truth is that underneath them all is profound peace. To fall into this peace we need to move beyond our initial emotional response and allow the process which will free us from the emotional roller coaster. By taking some quiet time alone you can explore your emotions, allow them and experience the layers. Remember that underneath everything is profound peace, don't get hooked on this though as it can become a block, because instead of being with where we are, we are instead focused on reaching the peace. Be gentle on yourself, relax, the peace will come. This processing is a skill and you will get better and better at it.

5. Breathe and invite expansion

Ask the Universe, God, The Divine (whatever you call it) to support you in staying with the uncomfortable feelings. There is a loving source that sustains us all....lets use it. Make a firm decision to see clearly whatever it is that you need to see. It may be where the pattern of your behaviour was first set, it may be seeing that you hold a limiting belief, it may be embracing something 'dark' that you have denied about yourself, such as your need to be right or your selfishness. I love these ones because they are usually triggered by someone else displaying the very behaviour I am in denial of. I see the other person and will think judgemental thoughts such as 'What a selfish git that person is'. The truth once revealed is always very funny. This is not to say that people don't act very selfishly or in other negative ways, but your assessment is your reaction to them. If you see the behaviour but are not emotionally triggered, you are in the clear. If on the other hand they drive you insane and make you really cross, it's time to look inside. Find some quiet space and then just allow whatever arises and seek not to judge it. This is of course a completely crazy request. How can we not judge something? Judging things is what we are programmed to do and it's a good thing. It can keep us safe and help us negotiate the world. On the flip side it can also be very limiting and keep us stuck. So by all means judge away but I invite you to see that it is a judgement and nothing more than that. It's not right or wrong, it's programmed by our society's code of living, by our parents or other influential people in our lives. Keep inviting the Universe to help you stay with the internal discomfort and don't forget to breathe.

6. Be Honest

Honesty is indeed the best policy. You don't have to tell the world, the most important thing is to be honest with yourself. So if you have done something 'wrong' (by your moral code and values) and it's really bugging you. Instead of trying to justify it just accept you did it wrong. It really is as simple as that. Our resistance is to ourselves. Remember my example of the bill I never paid and should have, as by my moral code and values, I was in the wrong.

You have to start from where you are. It's the only place to start. Sometimes we need to embrace parts of ourselves that we don't want to; i.e. all those things that we deem bad or unacceptable by the way we have been raised and conditioned by our society, our parents and our life experiences. The truth is we all have aspects of ourselves that we deny. I do, you do. We try and live up to this perfect example of our image of ourselves. Our idea of who we should be. For example, let's think about being selfish. What would jump into your head if I said to you "You are selfish"? For me, I instantly want to defend the **'fact'** that I'm not selfish. I might even begin to give you a list of all the self-sacrificing things that I do on a daily basis. The reality is though, that I am selfish sometimes, and actually it is a good thing.

We have a tendency to label emotions as good and bad. One of the main shifts in thinking comes from dropping this idea and instead beginning to allow and accept our emotions. This means that the suppressed emotions can be fully experienced and fully processed within ourselves. All too often we deny our emotions because they are considered 'bad'. We tell ourselves that we should not feel such a way, but if you feel a particular way then you owe it to yourself to acknowledge your feelings and accept them. This is the way to free yourself from the trappings of your conditioning. Remember that you have created the situation. Either because you have created it or you have allowed someone to treat you in a certain way. Honesty is important. I find increasingly that I have mixed emotions about things. When you try and pigeonhole into one category you are denying your own truth. It is fine to have mixed feelings. As you begin to know yourself, you begin to open to others and look at things from different perspectives. Also there is no one answer to anything. 'Facts are not facts, they are merely agreed fiction'. We all have a unique view of the world and this variety is one of the things that make life so wonderful.

Honesty assists openness. By being prepared to see whatever it is that we are in denial of, we find the freedom we are seeking. We all have 'good' and 'bad' bits of ourselves, but they are not really good and bad, they are born of judgement. They are society and time specific, you only have to look back through history to see the truth of this.

7. Be Open

Choose to be open to the process. Openness invites the Universe in to help you. If we only think in the way we have always thought we will not achieve new things, we will just create more of the same. If, however, we choose to be open to life, new ideas, insights and inspiration become available to us.

When we are faced with problems and attempt to solve them, the common way is to draw on what we already know. This does not create the space for new insight. In order to open yourself to new possibilities, accept that you don't know, and make the decision to 'see' a new way. Making this decision will open your awareness to something new. Everything starts with awareness. This may be difficult to grasp because we cannot understand the power of the universe with our minds. The best way to grasp it is to have a direct experience of it for yourself. So, make that choice, decide to let the universe into your life. Decide to open to the infinite possibilities that are available to us all.

Core Principles and Emotional Processing in Action

I was on a silent retreat with my friend and we had been asked to not contact family members unless it was essential. The point of the silence was to get inside yourself and explore, so if you contact family or friends you bring your awareness back outside. Being in a new relationship and after initially thinking I wouldn't contact him, I found it really hard not to and so was texting him once or twice a day. On one of the days I said something to my friend that he had said, and she said "Don't take this the wrong way, but why do you feel the need to contact him?"

My initial physical reaction was nausea, I felt like I'd been told off! I went off and firstly started to make her wrong 'She's always got something to say', then I went to justification 'It's fine to call him, what does it matter'. Can you see the resistance? These internal mental ramblings carried on for a bit before I finally took responsibility and started feeling my feelings. Yuck! It didn't feel good at all.
It took some effort to keep returning to the feelings and allowing them. I followed the sensations in my body and breathed deeply (this helps energy/emotions move). Before I had gone away I had been exploring being insecure and needy with intimate partners. I really wanted to change both my feelings and behaviour around it because it caused me problems. Having gone into this new relationship I didn't want to ruin it. I'd really shifted some things, through observation of my thinking and looking at the accuracy of it. What I often saw was that I created a huge, and I may add totally incorrect,

story around what I may have thought was going on. Amazing the rubbish we will generate to be congruent with our internal state.

Anyway back to the emotional processing, after spending some time feeling, which was interspersed with thoughts about not being insecure and not wanting to be insecure (more resistance) all of a sudden this thought popped into my head…

'You have been insecure in every other relationship you have been in, why should this one be any different?'

The thing was, instead of being a bad thing this struck me as completely hilarious. "So what?" I thought. It really didn't matter. I had spent my whole life trying not to be insecure because in my book it was a 'bad' thing. I felt really happy about it and really didn't, and don't mind if I'm insecure forever.

Later that day I felt no compulsion to text, I didn't need to. It was like all the energy had been taken out of a burning desire. I didn't feel needy or see it in my behaviour. Every now and then I think 'needy' thoughts and so I seek the truth, I just love and accept them and see them for what they are.

Although this inner journey can be challenging and uncomfortable, I urge you to do it, because once you learn how to fully allow your inner feelings and are prepared to accept whatever they are, liberation will follow. The greatest thing is that the very thing you have kept pushed down inside because it seems so 'bad' that you just don't want to face it, can become hysterically funny, (such as my insecurity), or peaceful, (such as the example below). When feelings are fully allowed, a wonderful and spontaneous natural melting comes. The very thing you have been hiding from yourself, is effortlessly no longer a problem for you, and will no longer impact on your behaviour.

A personal experience

I had an event where an emotion came up before I could attach a memory to it. I was doing a breathing exercise in a group situation. We were told to breathe deeply into our abdomen and the breathing got faster and faster. The first time I got to a point where it made me feel slightly uncomfortable and I didn't like it, so I slowed down. After this attempt we shared how we had felt. I shared and was told to just go with it, as nothing bad would happen.

I did and this really powerful feeling of fear came up. As I was thinking to myself what's that about? I suddenly had this vivid memory of being in hospital. I had been on a ventilator but this had been stopped and I had an oxygen mask on permanently. The memory came back where the nurses had rolled me and the mask fell off. I went into real panic as I thought I couldn't breathe without it. The whole thing made complete sense to me. I had connected this feeling of being short of breath with the fear of dying.

Don't be a victim of life, seek the learning in your experiences. If you view your life in this way when an event has not gone as you would have liked you will be able to see it for what it is and move forward instead of being left feeling disappointed and full of regret.

Liberation

"Until you make the unconscious conscious, it will direct your life and you will call it fate." Carl Jung

In 2007 Oneness Blessing came into my life via my wonderful friend, Edina, and I am so grateful for its fabulous gift. Oneness Blessing is a channelling of divine energy to expand consciousness and invoke the awareness of oneness, the connection of all life. Founded by Sri Bhagavan and Sri Amma, Oneness Blessing helps us to deepen our relationship with those we love, with ourselves, with strangers and with our creator. It also helps in the healing of the body and in the discharge of unhelpful repetitive emotional patterns, resulting in greater ease and comfort with oneself.

My initial experience of receiving it was so amazing, because my mind shut up and was really quiet. At the time I was in emotional turmoil about the breakdown of my relationship with my husband and I was churning over and over with the same old thoughts. Yet after receiving the blessing it felt like my mind had been switched off. It was such a relief. It did come back after a couple of days, but that experience of peace was perfect. The sessions were run from a local Oneness Blessing Givers house and having enjoyed the benefits so much I went back and received more. I found a growing internal peace and in September 2007 Edina and I went to Penninghame House in Scotland to do a week intensive Oneness Blessing Process. The week was transforming for me. At the end of it I felt so free. We left on my birthday, which felt so apt because I did feel like I had been reborn.

Easter 2008 saw Edina and I travelling to Chennai, India to The Oneness University for the Level 1 process. It was awesome! A truly remarkable experience. The Dasas (teachers) are some of the most beautiful beings I have ever met, their eyes radiate love and to be in their presence is an honour. Bhagavan and Amma were not present, they have taken a step back to lower the hype, but their pictures were up and I sensed their presence. I had felt an instant connection with Bhagavan but not so much with Amma and throughout the week I had heard several people saying about Amma the divine mother. The day we left I was waiting for Edina in a café when I gradually came to realise that The Divine Mother had entered my consciousness. She had done it so gently. As I realised I felt so happy, I went to the toilet and was aware of her presence. As I was sitting on the toilet, I felt her presence so strongly and she blessed me. Part of me was aware I was sitting on the toilet and my mind was thinking 'I'm on the toilet, surely there are more sacred places to receive a blessing'! And yet another part of me was moved to tears. I felt so much love, so much love for me. I found to be in the presence of another who had no judgement of me, only pure loving acceptance was such a beautiful experience. It was like it somehow melted all my self judgements and criticisms. Thank you to everyone who is a part of The Oneness University but a special thank you to Graham and Edina for making it possible for me.

The only way out is through.

The challenge is to take responsibility for your own feelings and not project them out onto someone else. All feelings/emotions are a natural response to life, a response which is born of our conditioning and life experiences, so anyone that really annoys us or challenges us offers the most perfect gift. 'WHAT?' I hear you yell. Yes, you heard me right. Those special individuals who push our buttons offer us the gift of personal growth, release from limiting beliefs. This is one of the most challenging aspects, but also one of the most rewarding. So make the choice to open to both those who push your buttons and the emotional response that you probably don't want to feel.

On a course I attended, there was one woman who I didn't like. Initially, I didn't think anything of it but one day I suddenly thought, "Why don't I like this lady, she hasn't done anything to me and I know nothing about her?" It occurred to me that it was completely irrational not to like this woman as I had no experience to confirm my feelings towards her. Then I realised something, she looked really similar to someone I had fallen out with in the past. This fascinated me, how I had projected a past experience onto someone I did not know. My feelings were nothing to do with her, they were feelings of discomfort from the past. She gifted me the opportunity to feel and become free from an old emotional charge.

Bhagavan says "anything fully experienced becomes bliss", even the most intense pain. So far I have found this to be true. The difficulty is in allowing yourself to submerge into it, rather than avoid it.

Once you take this brave and life changing step of personal responsibility you may need to understand the root of the emotions or you may not. It may be that the decision to leave the past behind is enough to release it and you do not need to emotionally connect with the experience. Alternatively, you may need to dive into the feeling and fully allow it to be felt in order for the energy held in your system to be dis-charged (remember the cycle of blame). Fully feeling your feelings will set you free. There is no time limit on how long you need to feel feelings for, it's a bit like asking, 'how long is a piece of string?' The timing is up to you, when you are fully in the flow with no resistance, the energy of feelings moves very rapidly. It is our resistance which may cause it to go on for a long time. Often, we may think we are fully allowing our feelings, but actually we are resisting them. A key indicator is: if you don't want to be feeling it, or are focusing on getting through it and feeling something else, this is a clear indication of resistance. Basically, when you completely accept and are completely content with whatever the feeling is, that's when total release comes.

When we can do this, we are able to embrace life's triggers and be grateful for them. Although challenging, they offer the greatest of rewards…liberation and freedom. This is not about happy clappy, life is a bed of roses, because inevitably challenging things will happen in life. However, once you know how to process your emotions you will be equipped with the tools to deal effectively, and as easily as possible, with anything that comes your way.

Try the opposite

I recently discovered an amazing technique that works really well. It's the complete opposite to a positive affirmation.

Take the thing that you are in denial of. Being needy, selfish, fat, shy, insecure .... anything whatever it is.

Let's use needy as an example. Say to yourself "I am needy" and observe your body reaction, allow whatever is there using the 7 steps. **WARNING:** Watch out for your story. Don't buy into it. Feel the feelings and sensations in the body. Breathe. If it doesn't move quickly on some level you are resisting. In the spirit of acceptance, just accept that you are resisting and be with that.

Keep repeating it to yourself and just watch what happens.

I have been using this myself and with clients and it's really powerful. I think that affirmations work to a point but are in direct conflict with the truth of what is in the moment.

Once we can fully allow the truth, our truth in that moment (even though that truth may be a fallacy) the whole thing moves.

I'll share an example. I have been exploring money recently and the flow of it in my life. One of the things I discovered was that in order to have money in abundance I have to be open to receive.

Having feisty independent traits and an attitude of 'it's best to do it myself', it becomes clear that I am not very open to receive.

On this discovery I went straight for a positive affirmation. "I am open to receive". The thing was this just made me feel really sad. I then thought I needed to process my sadness so I allowed the feelings, followed the 7 steps. It stayed and would not budge. I thought I must be resisting something and just allowed it to be kicking around in my awareness.

The next morning I woke early (I often get great insights in the morning) and knew that I was telling myself an untruth. The truth was I was not open to receive. So I switched it. I began to say to myself "I am not open to receive". Instant deep sadness, which I felt and it dissolved very quickly into humour and me feeling quite happy about not being open to receive.

Now I can happily say "I am open to receive" and it feels great, it feels like the truth.

One thing I was aware of as one of my blocks was not being able to ask. This is very limiting because we can only achieve so much by ourselves....the whole is greater than the sum of its parts. This difficulty with asking extended into other areas as well and was also a serious block to my business because I found it really hard to ask for business. This is obviously severely limiting but the power of it was almost like a paralysis. I found it so hard, a mammoth hurdle of discomfort to overcome every time I was faced with having to ask.

These unconscious aspects control your behaviour. While you are unconscious you will not notice this but once you raise your awareness you will begin to see it. They control you because you live as if they are the truth and tailor your behaviour around this. Miracles happen once you embrace them and effortless behaviour change.

Just like when I embraced the insecure aspect of myself that I was denying, I see differences in how I am behaving, thinking and feeling. I have been asking a lot more, have already received more and undoubtedly will continue to receive more.

I am watching now to see what happens and enjoying my new found freedom of being able to accept love, support and business!

Chapter 4

The Power of Belief

Evaluating Belief

Whatever belief you hold, examine it with an open mind and heart and ask whether it holds true. It is important to be honest with yourself. All too often we come across conflicting evidence that we dismiss because it doesn't hold with our belief. We must look at all evidence offered and evaluate it, not be selective. The search for truth involves harmonising heart and mind. Be still and present and contemplate your beliefs, balancing rational thought and feelings. It takes effort to change a belief, because they are habits. False beliefs create dysfunctional thinking, which create dysfunctional lives.

Acceptance/Forgiveness

Another tool to learn is the art of forgiveness, for both yourself and others. I have found that acceptance is the key, that when something is fully accepted it kind of melts away and forgiveness becomes almost unnecessary, as there is nothing to forgive. In all events that happen in our lives we do the best we can at that particular time, with the knowledge that we have at the time. It is very easy to see things differently with hindsight and then punish yourself for not realising this or that. Or it goes round and round as you try to justify it in some way in an attempt to avoid that dreaded internal discomfort. Use the 7 steps to process past events by allowing your feelings. Feeling the feelings is the only way through. Try it with something you have been denying as a bad thing, something you have done wrong (by your standards) but have been trying to justify in some way to make it ok. You will find that when you embrace it as wrong, the internal discomfort goes and you feel great. Your energy will begin to move again and you will feel invigorated. So if you have past mistakes that you are fretting over just be honest with yourself, acknowledge where you were wrong and perhaps could have done something differently, accept it, forgive yourself and move on. You do not need to actually physically apologise to a person to do this, although you may if you wish. The act of apologising with sincerity of heart is sufficient.

Learn to Love Yourself

I don't mean love yourself in a conceited or vain way but in a pure, happy way. Have unconditional love for yourself. Accept yourself completely, 'good' and 'bad' qualities. When you are able to fully embrace yourself and have unconditional love for yourself then you are able to have unconditional love for others. Pure love is the key to happiness.

We are all beautiful beings no matter what our external or internal appearance. What do you love about yourself? If you find love too strong, how about like!

What do I love about myself?

I love my physical body, not from a western beauty way though, as I am incredibly scarred with lots of grafted skin, but I love it because it is wonderful. As I said I have a piece of my thigh over my stomach because I lost muscle there and I guess I look quite freaky to the unfamiliar eye. But what a phenomenal thing my body is. How clever that it managed to heal itself from all that decay (with the aid of some amazing medical help). I love and appreciate my body, it may not be visually 'perfect' (perfection is perception) but without it I would not be here, it is my vehicle. It has taken me time to learn to love my body, it has been a real battle and the cause of many tears. The first time I saw my body naked after being ill I sobbed and sobbed and couldn't imagine ever being happy with myself or how anyone would ever find me attractive. Yet here I am 8 years on, happy with myself, I feel attractive and I am in a wonderful relationship, where I am loved and fancied.

I'm strong minded (this is double-edged, sometimes I don't love this part of myself). But let's not think in terms of good and bad, perhaps it would be better to think of it in terms of productive and unproductive. There are times when being strong minded is productive and times when it can be unproductive. This is fine, the trick is to know yourself. The key words here are honesty and acceptance. It is about learning to love yourself for who you are.

I'm funny, intelligent, witty, thoughtful.... most of the time! (Laughing to myself here). It is really hard to write a list like this without feeling conceited. All part of my conditioning!

Basically, what I wish to say is whatever you love about yourself build on and, whatever you don't love, accept. By accepting it and seeing it for what it is, something transformational will happen. You may feel that certain behaviour or things are just the way you are and you are unable to change. I don't believe that this is true. If you really choose to change something about yourself, then you can but you have to start by accepting it first. Change may occur either physically, emotionally, or your belief or perception may alter. These things are all intertwined. It doesn't have to be traumatic either, as healing takes place on many levels, some of which are outside of your conscious mind.

Positivity breeds positivity, and negativity breeds negativity. The more we can begin to feel positive about ourselves, the more that positivity will grow. Whatever you believe about yourself is just that, a belief and beliefs can be changed. So if you feel negative about yourself now you can change that. Make the decision right now to be kind to yourself. In the true spirit of acceptance, if this is really challenging for you, merely accept that this is where you are. **Awareness is the key to any change.**

What sort of person are you?

What beliefs do you hold about yourself?

List 10 initial thoughts that come into your head. **Do the list now; do not give it too much thought just list things that spontaneously come to mind.**

Did you do it? Or did you just skip to this bit ☺

If you did, are they positive or negative? Do you accept them?

If you want real insight into yourself make 2 lists:

1. The sort of person you think you are, qualities, values etc.
2. The sort of person you definitely are not, qualities, values etc.

Put the lists somewhere safe and every now and then, take a couple of the qualities and observe your behaviour and thinking for the day. I wonder if you will find things on the NOT list that sneak in?

REMEMBER

BE KIND TO YOURSELF. This stuff is about liberation and freedom NOT personal punishment. This is your exploration of yourself. It is about personal growth and expansion. It's not about judging ourselves against others, or being right or wrong.

Chapter 5

Our Power to Create.

Sometime ago I drew out the cycle of life creation, as follows.

The Cycle of Life Creation

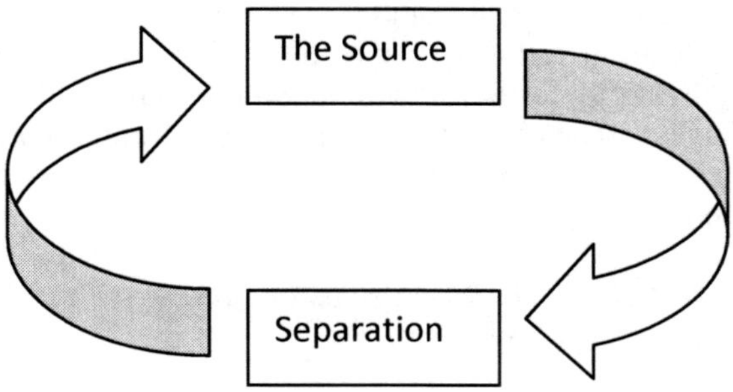

This is it! When this came from the pen in my hand I had a complete eureka moment. 'That's it, that's the point of life', I thought. Through the cycle there is Unity moving towards separation and then from the separation movement back towards unity. I think we are on a returning to the source phase with an ever increasing awareness of unity.

Just what do I mean by this? This is a bit of a cosmic statement and one that I can't really understand with my thinking mind. You see, the truth is much of this we cannot understand with our thinking minds but the habit is to continue to try to do so. It's quite funny really.

Just who are we? Who are you? Who am I?

When I was first asked this question I immediately answered with all the things I thought I was. For example, I'm a mother, a partner, a banker, baker, solicitor (insert whatever profession you are in), a daughter, a human being, a woman, a virgo etc. My experience is that I am all of those things and equally none of those things.

Just who we are is an amazing question to ponder and explore. This is a nice exercise to do. Sit quietly and ask yourself "Who am I?" Allow whatever comes to mind and then ask again. Just keep repeating the question as you peel back the layers.

My experience is that I am consciousness, so are you, we all are. We are here to experience life. I think we should all be fully living joyful lives that are complete and fulfilled. This fulfilment comes from nourishing relationships, new experiences, and knowing and experiencing the limitless potential that we really are.

Just what stops this? What stops us flowing with life, loving life and having a ball?

"So you will have died** before you die, **and then it won't matter anyway." *Ram Dass*

Ram Dass speaks here of the part of us that thinks we are something separate. This part of me that has the need to defend and protect itself, that needs to be right, wants to do well, yearns to be successful and loves the drama of life. Aren't so many of us just hooked into this? I see it as putting sticks on a fire. It feels good to have the choice of whether I add to the fire or decide to just be quiet and of course a fire with no fuel will die out.

I think he means that when we let go of being something separate and wake up to the connectedness that is us, that is all there is, then we have already died and gone to heaven. This is fully living, fully experiencing life because you are life. No boundaries and no limitations.

We are consciousness, therefore we are everything. Paradoxically the more we fully embrace everything (all those aspects we deny like anger, hate, fear etc) the more peaceful and loving we naturally become.

Perhaps the biggest 'battle' is the one within us, that ongoing inner battle with all the negative mind chatter that puts us down and holds us back. The only thing that really stops us doing or achieving anything is us. What if that's really true?

I remember when The Secret came out. It really struck a chord with me. The idea of the Law of Attraction and that our thoughts create our realities. Could it really be that easy? That what I focus on with my thoughts comes to me?

I have loved playing with it all. I think some of my resistance is to the simplicity of it. It's exactly like the emotions. All you need to do is embrace whatever is there. It's so easy and paradoxically so difficult. Perhaps because we have struggled for so long, suffered so much heartache and pain, an easy solution just doesn't cut it ☺ What do you think?

Thoughts are Powerful Things

"Live out of your imagination, not your history".
Stephen Covey

Just how many thoughts we have every day is debatable but it's a lot! Many of them seem to pop into my head rather than me specifically thinking about them. Quite clearly there is much here that we do not yet understand. What I have observed, however, is the more positively I think... then the more positively I think, the better I feel and the more readily good things happen. I have also observed that when I am thinking negative thoughts, I think more negative thoughts, I feel yuck and naff things happen. I often laugh at myself though because when naff things happen and I am in a really good mood they don't matter. So perhaps it's more a case of perception ☺

I love Stephen Covey's quote because much of our thought is mindless repetition of what we already know. We don't dare to dream for the fear of disappointment if it doesn't take shape. Give yourself permission to go for it! To dare to dream. We all know that it is imagination that creates new things.

If you have big dreams, big ideas, big ambition and want to live a big life surround yourself with people who believe in you.

What can you do to create joy in your life, rewarding experiences and easy living?

Now I know how to process my emotions and move through my self-imposed blocks, it's challenging at times, but always rewarding, I am now exploring and playing with creating my reality.

I saw an article recently titled 'The Law of Frustration'. It really made me laugh because it can definitely be a bit like this.

I think one of the keys to The Law of Attraction working for us versus being frustrating for us, is our awareness of the underlying parts of ourselves that we are unaware of.

We have talked a lot about feelings/emotions. This is the bit I am talking about. The body is the language of the unconscious. When you can learn to 'listen' to your body you can start to understand whether you are in alignment unconsciously with whatever it is you are focusing your thoughts on and trying to attract into your life. This 'physical intelligence' offers us the wisdom and liberation we are seeking. We all hold many false beliefs about ourselves, these false beliefs (lies) are born of our past experiences and can seriously limit us. Certain things like not feeling worthy or good enough but also denial of half of ourselves.

In our world of duality we believe that some things are good and some things are bad. The truth is everything just is and if we are consciousness we are in fact everything. I have the capacity to be both good and bad, evil and kind, independent and dependent, confident and shy and so on. Yet we deny many aspects as being 'bad'. This is a large part of the resistance that we talked about earlier. You have to start with where you are. I think this is sometimes why the Law of Attraction doesn't work for us because we are so focused on where we want to be and start getting frustrated that we are not there already. Where we are right now is absolutely perfect to highlight our unconscious to us and clear any limitations we have imposed on ourselves.

1. Start with embracing where you are right now.
2. Imagine where you would like to be, feel it, enjoy it.
3. Come back to the present and live in the moment.

I find more and more that it is never really 'things' I am after, the one true consistent aspect I am seeking is a feeling....feeling great that is ☺ The external circumstances don't seem so important and it amazes me how I can feel down and think it's about something outside of me but shortly afterwards feel great and be completely not bothered about the external circumstances even though they are exactly the same!

Our physical intelligence offers us the connection to the energy within our physical bodies and the ability to 'tune into' others on a deep level. I always get so excited about the potential of energy and our understanding of it. Once we start to interact on an energetic level it is so cool because it cuts through any lies. The lies that we are telling ourselves or put more simply the hidden truths that stop you and me expressing our full potential and being all that we can be. Also the lies that we tell each other, you know and probably experience this already. That inbuilt 'bullsh*t' detector! We all have it. We can all sense the incongruence when someone is telling us something that doesn't ring true. The more you practice stillness and expanding your awareness the more this ability will develop. It's not some weird psychic phenomena, it is simply the energy of all that is. Birds use magnetic fields to navigate, why shouldn't we use these same energetic fields to communicate?

A word of caution, you need to be careful with this subtle communication that you are not making assumptions about the other person that are revealing something to you about yourself.

"Everything that irritates us about others can lead us to an understanding of ourselves." Carl Jung

If something irritates you about someone else this is revealing something to you about you. **It is not about the other person.** Use the emotional processing to allow the insight to be revealed.

Learning how to fully process emotions frees up your energy and opens a space for you to begin to clearly see what is really happening rather than what you 'think' is happening. This is a vital aspect in creating your reality, because it is not just your conscious thoughts that create your reality, but the unconscious feelings and beliefs that add the power to those thoughts. You can focus your thoughts forever on something but if you unconsciously believe that you cannot have it for any reason (i.e. you are not in alignment with it) then it won't happen for you. You will begin to think that the Law of Attraction is indeed The Law of Frustration, or a load of rubbish and return to your less powerful self.

Once in alignment you can take up the pen in your hand and become the author of your own story. Flowing with life and allowing the universe to bring you everything you need.

Are you ready for a new world? For a new you? Are you ready to become the powerful loving presence that is the true you?

If you are it's simple.

1. Let go of everything you think you are.
2. Drop out of the drama (no more sticks on the fire).
3. Seek peace and cultivate that loving presence within you.
4. Have your big vision of what you would like to experience. **Focus on it every day without fail and have absolutely zero doubts that you can live it. Above all hold it....don't give up after a few weeks.**
5. Your body is your guide. Use your physical intelligence to process your unconscious blocks and expand your awareness.
6. **TAKE ACTION** on your inspired ideas and the opportunities that come your way.
7. **GET OUT OF YOUR OWN WAY!**

Number 3 gets my vote as the most important aspect! **'cultivate that loving presence within you'**...it helps you do number 7 ☺

Enjoy the life that you have right now. Don't dwell in the past or seek to live in the future…just look around you now and see the things that you are grateful for. The thoughts, actions and decisions that you make right now will impact on your future.

Don't take life so seriously.

Pursue your dreams.

Love yourself.

I'll leave you with this ....

"If someone believes in you, and you believe in your dreams, it can happen." Tiffany Loren Rowe.

I believe in you!

Exercises

Freedom from the past, Power in the Present.

1. **Conscious Breath**

   Breathing consciously is a powerful tool. Inhale through your nose or mouth, expanding your stomach first and then allowing your chest to fill as deeply as you can (for a count of 4 seconds is good but by all means do longer if you are comfortable). Hold for a moment and then exhale fully (for slightly longer than you inhaled), chest first, then stomach. Try a count of 4 in and 7 out to start. You can extend this if it's comfortable. Do this breathing for 3-5 minutes and you will feel more relaxed and connected within yourself.
   The beauty is you don't have to put special time aside, as you can easily incorporate breathing awareness into anything you already do.

2. **Right Now!**

   Bring all your awareness to this exact moment. Absorb the noises, smells, sensations all around you. Take a deep breath and allow your body to relax as you exhale.

3. **The Finer Details**

   Focus on something and bring all your awareness to that thing. For example, look at a flower and bring all your awareness to your observation of the flower, see in great detail all the intricate qualities and design. From this state of presence your awareness will naturally expand.

4. **Slow Down**

Slowing down and do something that doesn't demand constant evaluation from your mind or physical body. Maybe a repetitive task, such as gardening, walking or cleaning (with your total attention on the task alone). Remember to breathe.

5. **Walking Awareness**

Slow down your pace when you are walking and bring your full awareness to every step you take.

6. **Who am I ?**

Sit quietly and ask yourself "Who am I?" Allow whatever comes to mind and then ask again. Keep repeating the question as you peel back the layers.

7. **Space**

Sit quietly and start to become aware of the space all around you. Start with the room you are in and keep expanding your awareness. The space above, below and all around you. From the room, to outside the window, to the street, fields, county, country, sea, world, space and so on. Then bring yourself back through the expansions to the room and your body.

8. **Perfection of what is.**

Take the thing that you are in denial of. Being needy, selfish, fat, shy, insecure .... anything whatever it is. Repeat it to yourself and use the 7 steps to dissolve the charge

Let's use needy as an example. Say to yourself "I am needy" and observe your body reaction, allow whatever is there using the 7 steps.
WARNING: Watch out for your story. Don't buy into

it. Feel the feelings and sensations in the body. Breathe. If it doesn't move quickly on some level you are resisting. In the spirit of acceptance, just accept that you are resisting and be with that. Keep repeating it to yourself and just watch what happens.

9. **What beliefs do you hold about yourself?**

   List 10 initial thoughts that come into your head. Do not give it too much thought just list things that spontaneously come to mind.

10. **The Gift of Challenge**

    Start with embracing where you are right now. Switch your thinking to see your challenges as gifts. This is the first step to any change.

11. **A to the G**

    Practice an attitude of gratitude. Every morning list 5 things you are grateful for. Write them down and share them with someone if you can. Make this a daily practice.

12. **Feel the Groove**

    Move! Movement is fantastic for changing how you feel. Dance, stretch, rotate your joints. Breathe nice and deeply and feel how pleasurable it is. Be gentle and take it slow if you don't normally do it. This is not a competition it's about you, your own awareness and making your connection with your physical body so you can hear your physical intelligence.
    Build it up and aim for at least 15 minutes a day. Your 15 minutes to magic!

Quotation Sources

"Suffering is not in the fact, it is in the perception of the fact". Sri Bhagavan

www.onenessuniversity.org

"No one can make you feel inferior without your consent". Eleanor Roosevelt (1937) 15

http://en.wikiquote.org/wiki/Eleanor_Roosevelt

"Until you make the unconscious conscious, it will direct your life and you will call it fate." Carl Jung 30

http://www.trans4mind.com/counterpoint/tan3.shtml

"So you will have died before you die, and then it won't matter anyway." Ram Dass 42

http://www.gaytoday.com/garchive/people/090297pe.htm

"Live out of your imagination, not your history". Stephen Covey 43

http://thinkexist.com/quotation/live_out_of_your_imagination-not_your_history/218940.html

"Everything that irritates us about others can lead us to an understanding of ourselves." Carl Jung 46

http://thinkexist.com/quotation/everything_that_irritates_us_about_others_can/8704.html

"If someone believes in you, and you believe in your dreams, it can happen." Tiffany Loren Rowe. 47

I Believe In You. Compiled by Dan Zadra. 2009.

Also from MX Publishing

Seeing Spells Achieving

The UK's leading NLP book for learning difficulties including dyslexia

Stop Bedwetting in 7 Days

A simple step-by-step guide to help children conquer bedwetting problems in just a few days

Recover Your Energy

NLP for Chronic Fatigue, ME and tiredness

More NLP books at www.mxpublishing.co.uk

Also from MX Publishing

Play Magic Golf

How to use self-hypnosis, meditation, Zen, universal laws, quantum energy, and the latest psychological and NLP techniques to be a better golfer

Psychobabble

A straight forward, plain English guide to the benefits of NLP

You Too Can Do Health

Improve Your Health and Wellbeing, Through the Inspiration of One Person's Journey of Self-development and Self-awareness Using NLP, energy and the Secret Law of Attraction

More NLP books at www.mxpublishing.co.uk

Lightning Source UK Ltd.
Milton Keynes UK
08 August 2010

158063UK00001B/24/P

9 781907 685033